SUPER
SANDCASTLE·
Poetry Power

BEES ~TO~ TREES

Reading, Writing, and Reciting
Poems About Nature

COMPILED & EDITED BY SUSAN M. FREESE   ILLUSTRATED BY JAN WESTBERG

ABDO
Publishing Company

Published by ABDO Publishing Company, 8000 West 78th Street,
Edina, MN 55439. Copyright © 2008 by Abdo Consulting Group, Inc.
International copyrights reserved in all countries. No part of this book may
be reproduced in any form without written permission from the publisher.
Super SandCastle™ is a trademark and logo of ABDO Publishing Company.

Printed in the United States.

Editor: Pam Price
Curriculum Coordinator: Nancy Tuminelly
Cover and Interior Design and Production: Mighty Media

Library of Congress Cataloging-in-Publication Data

Freese, Susan M., 1958-
  Bees to trees : reading, writing, and reciting poems about nature /
  Susan M. Freese.
     p. cm.
  Includes index.
  ISBN 978-1-60453-001-8
1. Poetry--Authorship--Juvenile literature. 2. Children's poetry, American.
3. Nature in literature. I. Title.

PN1059.A9F742 2008
808.1--dc22

                          2007037589

Super SandCastle™ books are created by a team of professional educators,
reading specialists, and content developers around five essential components—
phonemic awareness, phonics, vocabulary, text comprehension, and fluency—
to assist young readers as they develop reading skills and strategies and increase
their general knowledge. All books are written, reviewed, and leveled for guided
reading, early intervention reading, and Accelerated Reader® programs for use
in shared, guided, and independent reading and writing activities to support a
balanced approach to literacy instruction.

About SUPER SANDCASTLE™

Bigger Books for Emerging Readers Grades PreK–3

Created for library, classroom, and at-home
use, Super SandCastle™ books support and
engage young readers as they develop and
build literacy skills and will increase their
general knowledge about the world around
them. Super SandCastle™ books are part of
SandCastle™, the leading preK–3 imprint for
emerging and beginning readers. Super
SandCastle™ features a larger trim size for
more reading fun.

Let Us Know

Super SandCastle™ would like to hear
your stories about reading this book.
What was your favorite page? Was
there something hard that you needed
help with? Share the ups and downs of
learning to read. We want to hear from
you! Send us an e-mail.
sandcastle@abdopublishing.com

Contact us for a complete list of SandCastle™,
Super SandCastle™, and other nonfiction and fiction
titles from ABDO Publishing Company.
www.abdopublishing.com
8000 West 78th Street Edina, MN 55439
800-800-1312 · 952-831-1632 fax

A Note to Librarians, Teachers, and Parents

The poems in this book are grouped into three sections. "I Can Read" has poems that children can read on their own. "Read With Me" has poems that may require some reading help. "Kids' Corner" has poems written by children.

There are some words in these poems that young readers may not know. Some of these words are in boldface. Their pronunciations and definitions are given in the text. Other words can be looked up in the book's glossary.

When possible, children should first read each poem out loud. That way they will hear all of the sounds and feel all of the rhythms. If it is not possible to read aloud, instruct them to read the poems to themselves so they hear the words in their heads.

The **Poetry Pal** next to each poem explains how the poet uses words and specific styles or techniques to make the reader feel or know something.

The **Speak Up!** sidebar prompts readers to reflect on what they think each poem means and how it relates to them.

Become a Poet! provides ideas and activities to encourage and enhance learning about reading, writing, and reciting poetry.

Contents

What Is Poetry? 4
Seasons of Trees, Shania Ford 6

I Can Read 8
Busy Bee, Eileen Spinelli 10
When Clouds Meet, Eric Ode 12
Things to Do If You Are the Rain, Bobbi Katz 13
Haiku, Robert Pottle 14
In Praise of Tiny Things, Eileen Spinelli 15
Who Has Seen the Wind? Christina Rossetti 16
Windy Nights, Robert Louis Stevenson 17

Read With Me 18
Dragonfly, Georgia Heard 20
The Night, Myra Cohn Livingston 21
The Fog, Carl Sandburg 22
Breakers, Lillian Morrison 23
Spring Is, Bobbi Katz 24

Kids' Corner 26
Winter, Luis Cordero 26
Tiny Tiny Island, Kayla Vue 27

Become a Poet! 28

Glossary 30

Permissions 31

Index 32

What Is

Let's pretend someone has asked you to write about something in nature. Maybe you love clouds or flowers or beaches. But you have to follow these rules for writing. First, you can't use very many words. And second, you have to put the words in order so they make a rhyme or a rhythm when you read them.

These are some of the rules for writing poetry. Poetry is different from the writing you do at school and other places, which is called **prose** (PROZE). Here's how!

Poets, the people who write poetry, use fewer words than other kinds of writers. That means they have to pick just the right words to say what they think and feel. The words in poems often are about how things look, feel, smell, taste, and sound. Poets use words to paint pictures for their readers.

4

poetry?

Poets also arrange words in ways to create rhyme and rhythm. You probably know that words that **rhyme** (RIME) sound the same, such as *cat*, *sat*, and *bat*. Rhyming words are fun to say and to hear. A **rhythm** (RIH-thum) is a pattern of sounds. Think about the beat you feel when you clap or march to music. You can feel the same kind of beat when you read a poem. By using rhythm and rhyme, poets make words sound like music.

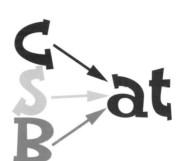

What else is special about poetry? Because of all the choices poets get to make when they write, no two poems are ever the same. You will see that when you read the poems in this book! And you will find that out when you write your own poems too!

Getting Started

The terms on
the next page tell
how poets
choose words
and put them
together in
special ways.
As you read
about each
term, look
at the poem
"Seasons of Trees"
to see an example.

Seasons of Trees

BY SHANIA FORD

The winter trees are brown and bare.
In spring, they green and grow.
The summer finds them fresh and full.
The fall leaves drop and blow.

line

A line in a poem is a group of words written across the page. In "Seasons of Trees," the first line is "The winter trees are brown and bare." Each new line starts below the one before it. There are four lines in this short poem.

stanza
(STAN-zuh)

A stanza is a group of lines in a poem that are usually about the same idea. A stanza is like a paragraph in other kinds of writing. Stanzas are separated by blank lines of space. "Seasons of Trees" has just one stanza.

rhyme
(RIME)

Words that rhyme end with the same sound, such as *dog* and *log* and *fox* and *socks*. In a poem, the last words of the lines often rhyme but not always. In many poems, every pair of lines rhymes or every other line rhymes. In "Seasons of Trees," lines 2 and 4 rhyme. Look at the words *grow* and *blow*.

rhythm
(RIH-thum)

Even poems that don't rhyme have rhythm, a pattern of sounds or beats. In most poems, some sounds are accented. That means you say them with a little more punch. Read "Seasons of Trees" aloud and listen to which sounds you accent. Clap on these sounds to help you hear and feel them. You probably read line 1 using a pattern like this, "The **WIN**-ter **TREES** are **BROWN** and **BARE**." To read this line, you accent every other sound, starting with the second one. There are four accented sounds, or beats, in this line. Line 2 has the same pattern of sounds but only three beats, "In **SPRING**, they **GREEN** and **GROW**." What about lines 3 and 4? Line 3 has the same rhythm as line 1, and line 4 has the same rhythm as line 2.

I Can Read

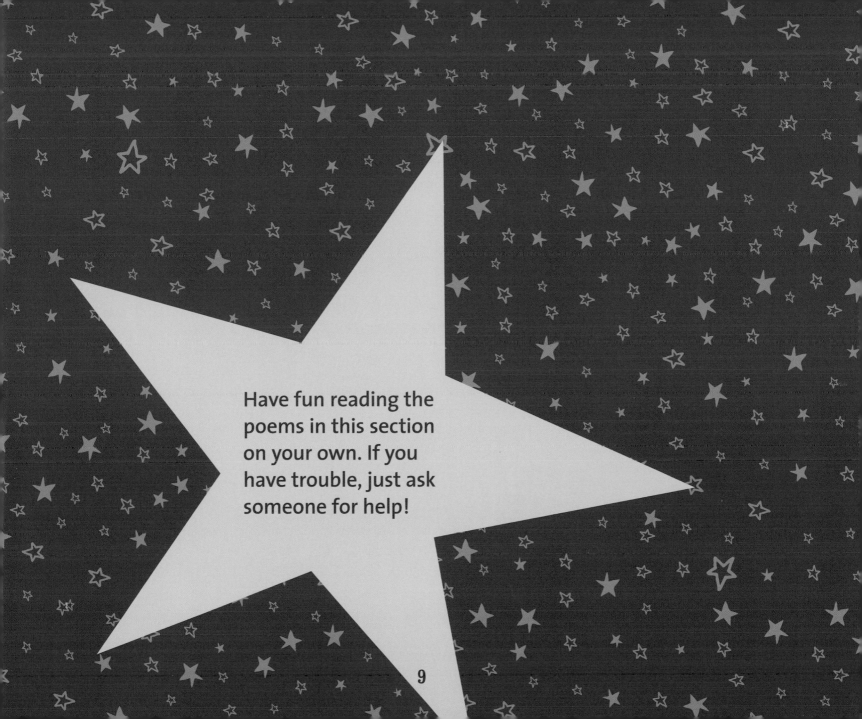

Have fun reading the poems in this section on your own. If you have trouble, just ask someone for help!

9

Busy Bee

BY EILEEN SPINELLI

Bee is busy in my garden
      buzzing round the mint and chive,
      sipping nectar from the roses,
      back and forth from bloom to hive.

Bee goes dancing deep in clover,
      visits my begonia bed,
      blossom shaking, honey-making—
      Bee has lots of work ahead.

I am buzzing round my garden,
    chasing beetles, shaking dirt,
    snipping sprigs of dill and parsley,
    giving thirsty ferns a squirt.

Back and forth from beans to peppers,
    set the basket on the shelf,
    sweep the path and heap the clippings—
    I'm a busy bee myself.

SPEAK UP!

Who do you know that
has a garden or grows
plants indoors? Why do
you think people like
to grow things?

11

POETRY PAL

This poem might seem funny to you, because it talks about clouds like they're people! Count how many things the clouds do that really only people can do.

Talking about things like they're people is called **personification** (purr-SAHN-iff-ih-KAY-shun). Poets use personification to make things seem alive.

SPEAK UP!

If clouds really were like people, what would they say to each other?

When clouds Meet

BY ERIC ODE

When one cloud meets another
on a cold and windy day,
do they smile and greet each other?
Do they have a lot to say?
Do they laugh when they're together?
Do they grumble and complain?
Do they talk about the weather?
Do they say, "It looks like rain"?

Things to Do If You Are the Rain

BY BOBBI KATZ

Be gentle.
Hide the edges of buildings.
Plip, plop in puddles.
Tap, tap, tap against the rooftops.
Sing your very own song!
Make the grass green.
Make the world smell special.
Race away on a gray cloud.
Sign your name with a rainbow.

POETRY PAL

This poem also uses personification. Here the speaker is talking to the rain like it's a person. The whole poem is a to-do list for the rain! Every line tells the rain something else to do, to sound like, to smell like, and so on.

This kind of list in a poem is called a **catalog** (CAT-uh-log).

SPEAK UP!

What's on your to-do list? What things are you supposed to do at home or school? What do you sometimes forget to do?

Haiku

BY ROBERT POTTLE

Snow bending the boughs
finally falls from the tree
and lands on my face.

14

In Praise of Tiny Things

BY EILEEN SPINELLI

A strawberry, a cowrie shell, an acorn from a tree.
A flake of snow, a seed to grow, a butterfly, a bee.
Meteor dust from distant stars, a hummingbird in flight.
A pebble and a daisy. A firefly at night.
A sea-horse and a spider. A simple grain of sand.
The world is full of wondrous things
much smaller than your hand.

15

POETRY PAL

Here's another poem about small things in nature. It's a list, or catalog, of tiny things that are **wondrous** (ONE-druss). That means they are so special they make us wonder about them. A poem that says why something is wonderful is called an **ode**.

Some of the most famous poems ever written are odes about nature.

SPEAK UP!

Make a list of four things in nature that are smaller than your hand. Why is each one wondrous?

POETRY PAL

Look at the two stanzas in this poem. They're almost the same, aren't they? Using the same words or lines over again is called **repetition** (rep-uh-TIH-shun). Poets use repetition to create rhythm. Read this poem aloud and listen to where you pause and where you punch the words a little.

SPEAK UP!

You can't see the wind, but you know when it's there. Think of something else that you can't see but know is real. How do you know?

Who Has Seen the Wind?

BY CHRISTINA ROSSETTI

Who has seen the wind?
    Neither I nor you:
But when the leaves hang trembling,
    The wind is passing through.

Who has seen the wind?
    Neither you nor I:
But when the leaves bow down their heads,
    The wind is passing by.

16

Windy Nights

BY ROBERT LOUIS STEVENSON

Whenever the moon and stars are set,
Whenever the wind is high,
All night long in the dark and wet,
    A man goes riding by.
Late in the night when the fires are out,
Why does he gallop and gallop about?

Whenever the trees are crying aloud,
    And ships are tossed at sea,
By, on the highway, low and loud,
    By at the gallop goes he;
By at the gallop he goes, and then
By he comes back at the gallop again.

POETRY PAL

This poem uses personification to talk about the wind like it's a man on a horse. He gallops about all night long, going here and there, back and forth.

The title of the poem gives a big clue to what it's about.

SPEAK UP!

Compare this poem with "Who Has Seen the Wind?" How are they alike? How are they different? Which one do you like the best? Why?

Read With Me

Enjoy reading these poems with someone who can help you with the harder words and ideas. Poetry is more fun when you understand what you are reading!

Dragonfly

BY GEORGIA HEARD

It skims the pond's surface,
searching for gnats, mosquitoes, and flies.
Outspread wings blur with speed.
It touches down
and stops to sun itself on the dock.
Wings flicker and still:
stained-glass windows
with sun shining through.

The Night

BY MYRA COHN LIVINGSTON

The night
    creeps in
    around my head
    and snuggles down
    upon the bed,
    and makes lace pictures
    on the wall
    but doesn't say a word at all.

POETRY PAL

If you didn't read the title or the first line of this poem, would you think it was about a cat? In lines 2 through 5, talking about the night as if it were a cat creates a **metaphor** (METT-uh-for). A metaphor describes something you already know about to help you understand something else. For example, what are the "lace pictures on the wall"?

SPEAK UP!

You probably guessed that the "lace pictures" are shadows. Do you think shadows are pretty or scary?

The Fog

BY CARL SANDBURG

The fog comes
on little cat feet.

It sits looking
over harbor and city
on silent haunches
and then moves on.

22

Breakers

BY LILLIAN MORRISON

Roaring,
all flowing grace,
the water tigers pounce,
feed on the shore,
worry it
again and again,
take great bites
they cannot swallow
and leave the toothmarks
of their long white fangs.

POETRY PAL

Breakers are big waves that crash on the shore. Maybe you figured that out when you read the words *water tigers* in line 3. This poem is another extended metaphor. It tells what waves are like by talking about what tigers are like. Which lines tell how waves wash away the sand and leave white foam on the shore?

SPEAK UP!

Like a tiger, nature can be very powerful. When have you seen nature damage or hurt things?

This poem doesn't look like other poems, does it? In each stanza, some of the lines look like stairs!

Read the poem out loud and listen to how you read these lines. You probably read them quickly and with a little extra punch. You probably read the other lines more slowly, pausing at the end of each one. How the poet arranges the words and lines on the page can create rhythm.

Spring Is

BY BOBBI KATZ

Spring is when
      the morning sputters like
bacon
    and
      your
        sneakers
          run
            down
              the
                stairs
so fast you can hardly keep up with them,
and

spring is when
      your scrambled eggs
          jump
              off
                  the
                      plate
and turn into a million daffodils
trembling in the sunshine.

25

SPEAK UP!

This poem uses words with a lot of energy. Things are running and jumping around! Spring seems fun and happy. What kinds of words would you use to write a poem about your favorite season?

Kids' Corner

What a perfect way to write a poem about winter! The words are falling from the sky like snowflakes. A poem that looks like what it's about is called a **concrete** (kahn-KREET) **poem.**

One way to write a concrete poem is to form the words into the shape of the subject. First, write down the words in lines or sentences. After you are sure of all the words, then put them in the right shape.

Winter

BY LUIS CORDERO

Winter

is so cold

but is fun too.

You can have hot cocoa when You are cold.

when You are cold.

snow covers everything with a blanket.

26

Tiny Tiny
Island

BY KAYLA VUE

Small beautiful all alone
with water all around
no other land to come and help
does it feel like it could drown?

Become a Poet!

Here are some activities to help you write your own poems.

Keep a Journal

Many writers keep a journal, which is a book of ideas, thoughts, and drawings. Start your own journal in an empty notebook. Write down ideas for your own poems. Write down things that happen, what you like and don't like. Keep your journal with you so you can use it often.

Learn New Words

In the back of your journal, make a list of new words you learn. Start with the words you learned while reading the poems in this book. Write down each word and what it means. Then write each word in a sentence to make sure you know how to use it. Also write down how to say it if you think you won't remember.

Make a Picture

Draw or paint a picture about one of the poems in this book. Maybe pick one of the poems that has many words about colors and other things you can see. Share both the poem and the picture with someone.

Write a Story

Choose one of the poems in this book and write a story from it. Your story can be about what's happening in the poem or who's in the poem. Write using your own words, not the words from the poem.

Have a Poetry Reading

With a few friends or family members, put on a show where everyone has a turn to read a poem out loud. When people aren't reading, they should be in the audience. Practice using correct rhythm and rhyme beforehand. Also make sure you know all the words. Try reciting the poem from memory, if you can.

Find More Poems

What's your favorite poem in this book? Who wrote it? Use the Internet and books in your library to find another poem by this poet. Read the new poem several times. Then read your favorite poem again. How are the two poems alike? How are they different? Which poem do you like best now? Write about the poems in your journal.

Learn About Poets

Use the Internet or books in your library to learn about famous poets. Start with Eileen Spinelli, who writes a lot of children's poems. Where is she from? What poems has she written? Read four poems by Eileen Spinelli and pick your favorite. Write down in your journal why you like this poem the best.

Make a Recording

Record yourself reading one of the poems from this book out loud. Practice so you can read the poem with the correct rhythm and rhyme. Ask your parent or teacher for help, if you need it. Record other poems later to make a set of your favorite poems.

Glossary

begonia – a type of flowering plant.

blur – to make it hard to clearly see the shape of something.

bough – a large branch of a tree.

clipping – something that has been clipped off of something else, such as branches cut from plants or trees.

flicker – to move quickly and unsteadily.

gallop – to run at the fastest speed possible.

grumble – to complain in a low voice.

haunches – the back legs of a four-legged animal.

heap – to pile up.

meteor – a bright streak of light caused by a small object entering the earth's atmosphere.

pounce – to jump suddenly on something in order to catch it.

skim – to move quickly over something.

sprig – a small twig or shoot of a tree or plant.

permissions

Index

Catalog, 13, 15

Concrete poem, 26, 27

Cordero, Luis, 26

Drawing (and poetry), 20, 26, 27, 28

Extended metaphor, 22, 23

Ford, Shania, 6

Haiku, 14

Heard, Georgia, 20

Journal writing, 27, 28, 29

Katz, Bobbi, 13, 24–25

Line, 7, 13, 14, 16, 21, 23, 24

Livingston, Myra Cohn, 21

Metaphor, 21, 22, 23

Morrison, Lillian, 23

Ode, 15

Ode, Eric, 12

Personification, 12, 13, 17

Poetry

    definition of, 4–5

    terms about, 5, 7

Poetry reading, 29

Poets, 4, 5, 29

Pottle, Robert, 14

Prose, 4

Recording (poetry reading), 29

Repetition, 16

Rhyme, 5, 7

Rhythm, 5, 7, 16, 24

Rossetti, Christina, 16

Sandburg, Carl, 22

Sensory details, 20

Speaker, 10, 13

Spinelli, Eileen, 10–11, 15, 29

Stanza, 7, 10, 16, 24

Stevenson, Robert Louis, 17

Stories (and poems), 28

Syllables, 14

Title, 17, 21

Vue, Kayla, 27

Word choices,
    4, 5, 6, 14, 16, 20, 25, 28